TIME FOR KIDS READERS

D1790157

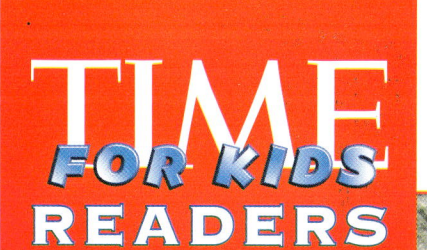

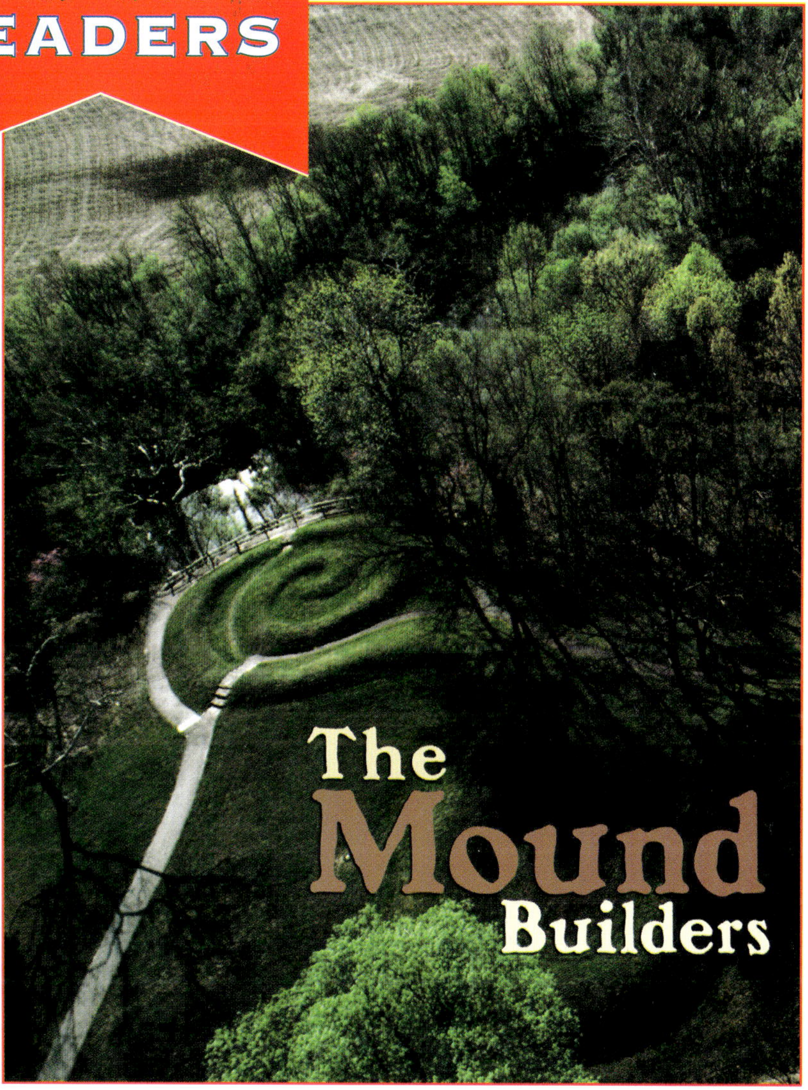

The Mound Builders

by Sheila Sweeny

Harcourt
SCHOOL PUBLISHERS

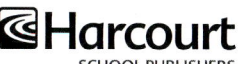

Orlando Austin New York San Diego Toronto London

Visit *The Learning Site!*
www.harcourtschool.com

Outside the city of Evansville, Indiana, a mystery waits to be solved. Standing near the Ohio River on more than 600 rolling acres are mounds and mounds of—well, mounds. They range in width from a few feet to dozens of yards.

Who built the mounds? From about A.D. 1100 to 1450, the site was a town of several thousand American Indians. They built the mounds. Experts have been studying these mounds for more than a century.

Today the site is called Angel Mounds, after the family that once had a farm there. Experts call the mounds *earthworks*. At one time, at least 200,000 such dirt structures stood in North America. Some were shaped like animals, such as snakes, bears, or birds. Others were circles, squares, or octagons. Some mounds stood alone on hilltops. Some stood one behind the other like a line of soldiers. Every group of mounds marks a place where a community of American Indians once lived.

Today, not many sites like Angel Mounds are left. One site is at Mounds State Park near Anderson, in central Indiana. There, ten awesome earthworks rise out of the ground. The largest one, the Great Mound, is shaped like an enclosed circle. It is 100 yards across—the length of a football field. Another mound, the Great Serpent Mound in Adams County, Ohio, is more than 1,300 feet in length—that's almost a quarter of a mile! American Indians built these mounds more than 2,000 years ago. But why? And how? Experts have some answers. They are working hard to find others.

The Great Serpent Mound

Who Were the Mound Builders?

Over the years people have had a lot of different ideas about the Mound Builders. Some said the builders were Vikings from northern Europe. Others said the builders were people from Atlantis, a so-called lost continent. Experts have proved these and other theories wrong.

Scientists have studied clues left behind at the mound sites. The clues helped give a picture of what life was like when the mounds were built. However, the story of humans in North America begins further back than that. It begins 12,000 years ago, during what many historians consider to be the last Ice Age.

During the Ice Age, sheets of ice covered much of Earth. The ice crept down from the Arctic. Some of the ice sheets were as much as 1 mile thick.

The sheets slid down as far as what is now central Indiana. South of the sheets of ice was tundra, or treeless plains. The surface of tundra thaws every summer. Beneath it is a layer of permafrost, or earth that stays frozen all year long.

People lived in small groups. For food, they gathered wild plants and berries and hunted animals, such as woolly mammoths, bison, and deer. The hunt for food forced these early American Indians to move their camps often.

Scientists call these people *Paleo-Indians*. Paleo-Indians had descended from the first people to live in North America, who came from Asia. They crossed to what is now Alaska on Beringia (buh•RIN•jee•uh), a bridge of land that is now underwater. Moving in search of food, their descendants spread over much of North America and South America.

Over a period of thousands of years, the ice sheets melted. The melted water raised the water level of the oceans. Water covered the land bridge from Asia, cutting it off from North America.

The land slowly changed. Woolly mammoths and giant bison began to disappear. The frozen tundra became prairie and forestland. Paleo-Indians adapted to the changes. Gathering roots and seeds became easier. Many people made their homes near rivers, where they could catch fish. Others stayed on the plains, where animals were plentiful. With more food to eat, more children lived to become adults.

Paleo-Indians hunted woolly mammoths for meat and for fur.

The Adena

Over time, each group of Paleo-Indians developed its own language, way of life, and religious beliefs. The groups grew from small bands to tribes and then to larger communities of tribes. Chiefs organized and led the tribes. Thousands of years later, their descendants began building mounds.

Scientists named the first mound builders in North America the *Adena*. Three thousand years ago, the Adena lived throughout what are now Indiana, Ohio, West Virginia, Kentucky, and parts of Pennsylvania and New York.

The Adena hunted, fished, and gathered plants for food. They also learned to grow sunflowers, squash, and other crops. Becoming farmers enabled them to settle in small villages. They built mounds and buried their dead in them. They may also have used the mounds for religious purposes. The Adena built shelters on some of the mounds, possibly homes for the chiefs or religious leaders.

An Adena burial mound

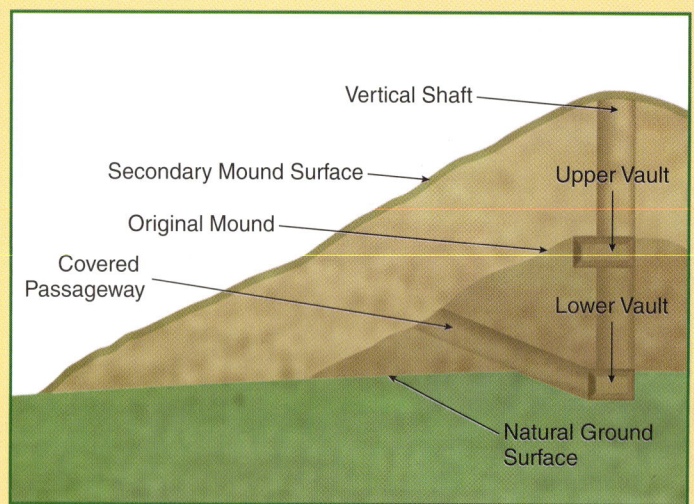

The mounds tell us a lot about the Adena. They were very good builders. They did everything by hand. They didn't have horses or wheelbarrows. They carried dirt in baskets to build the mounds. Scientists think that the biggest earthworks may have taken 100 years or more to build.

When burying their dead, the Adena usually cremated the bodies. Then they placed the ashes in log tombs that were covered with earth. Sometimes they buried objects they valued, such as mica and shells, with the dead.

These buried objects help us see how trade linked the American Indians. The copper found in some mounds came from the Great Lakes area. Shells came from the Gulf of Mexico. Mica, a shiny mineral, came from what are now North and South Carolina. The Adena could have traded directly with people from those areas. It's more likely, though, that the items were traded from owner to owner across the continent.

Adena spear points (right). This Adena statue (far right) is from the Woodland period (500 B.C. to A.D. 1). It was found in the early twentieth century at the Adena Mound in Ross County, Ohio.

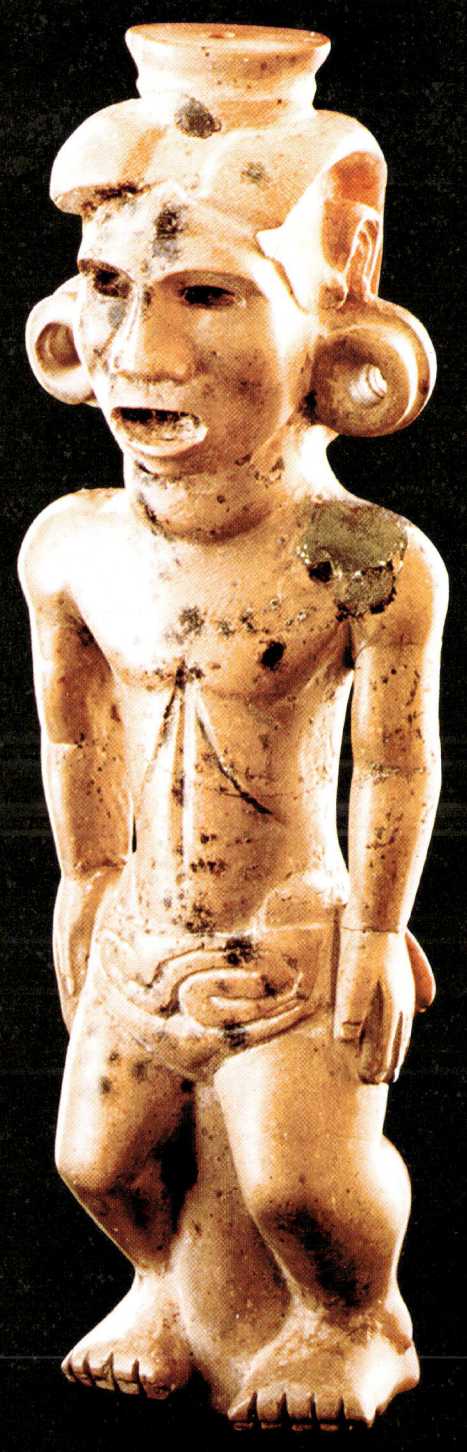

The Hopewell

The Hopewell, another group of American Indians, lived about 2,000 years ago. For awhile, the Hopewell lived side by side with the Adena. The Hopewell were also Mound Builders.

The Hopewell borrowed some ideas from the Adena and made them their own. Compared to the Adena, the Hopewell were wealthy. Hopewell burial mounds were also more complex, and their arts and crafts were more detailed.

The Hopewell built villages near rivers. The rich soil near the rivers helped their crops grow well. Like the Adena, the Hopewell hunted, fished, and gathered wild plants to eat. However, the Hopewell had better lives. Scientists say this is because of the way the Hopewell did their work. Many Hopewell developed specialized skills. One person might plan a structure, such as a home or a mound. Other people would then build it. Still other people were artists and traders. As in earlier times, the women farmed and the men hunted. When the seasons changed, the Hopewell moved their villages to new locations.

Like the Adena, the Hopewell buried their dead in mounds. Experts are studying the Hopewell mounds to see if they might have been used to mark certain natural events. The locations of some of the mounds may have helped the Hopewell identify the year's longest and shortest days. These days may have been important in the Hopewell religion.

A golf course was built over a circular Hopewell mound in Newark, Ohio.

The Hopewell buried many beautiful objects with their dead, as the Adena did. They believed that a person's spirit needed these things in the next world. The rarer the objects, the more important the person had been.

The Hopewell had to trade to get the materials to create many of these objects. They hammered copper nuggets into flat sheets. From the sheets, they formed tools and art objects. They decorated axes and headdresses with copper. The Hopewell also hammered iron, silver, and gold into useful things such as tools.

The Hopewell traded across most of North America. Experts have found the teeth of grizzly bears in Hopewell burial mounds. Those teeth came from the West. The teeth and jaws of alligators and sharks have also been found in burial mounds. These items must have come from the Southeast. They were traded from tribe to tribe until they reached the Midwest. Trade helped spread Hopewell culture as far away as what are now New York and Florida.

The Hopewell people did not have one main leader. Each village had its own chief and its own religious ceremonies. The Hopewell villages rarely had more than 400 people.

About 1,500 years ago, the Hopewell disappeared. No one knows exactly what happened. It's one more mystery that hasn't been solved. It would be at least 200 years until there were other Mound Builders.

The claw (below left) and the pot decorated with hands (below right) were made between 300 B.C. and A.D. 500 by the Hopewell.

These mounds are located within Hopewell Culture National Historic Park.

The Mississippians

A special way of life developed among the American Indians who lived in the Mississippi River valley. The Mississippians were Mound Builders. Their culture spread along much of this important river and lasted nearly 1,000 years.

The Mississippians were expert farmers. They used hoes to clear weeds and to break up soil. They used a new weapon, the bow and arrow, to hunt animals.

Because the Mississippians were farmers, they did not have to move from place to place searching for food. They formed long-lasting villages. The Mississippians even built an empire, or a vast territory run by a single group of leaders.

Mississippian culture spread east to today's Georgia, west to Texas, and north to Minnesota. Almost 40,000 people lived in one Mississippian city.

The Mississippians used baskets to move the dirt that became the mounds. Since there were so many people to do the work, their mounds were the biggest mounds ever built. One Mississippian mound is more than 100 feet high. It covers an area equal to the area of 30 football fields.

Angel Mounds, Indiana, provides a lot of information about the Mississippians. Thousands of people, including the chief, lived there between A.D. 1100 and 1450. A trench of logs and mud circled the town to protect it.

Angel Mounds was the center of a large community that stretched 70 miles in all directions. Angel Mounds was a center of trade, government, and religion. People traveled to Angel Mounds to exchange goods or to take part in religious ceremonies.

A mound (left) made by people of the Mississippian culture is at Toltec State Park, near Little Rock, Arkansas.

A village in Wisconsin built a stockade around a Mississippian mound-builder site called Aztalan.

People lived at Angel Mounds for more than 300 years. Then the site was abandoned. No one knows why. Some experts believe that the people of Angel Mounds died from a disease that spread very quickly.

Today, people visit Angel Mounds to see what is left of the great city. Visitors can imagine the Mississippians gathering at the mounds. They can imagine what a chief's home might have looked like. They can look across the land and see where the village cornfields might have been. Visitors might find a clue. They might even find a new mystery.

This statue of a possum's head was made by a Mississippian artist in about A.D. 1200.